Fact Finders®

WHAT WENT WRONG ?

The Triangle Shirtwaist Factory Fire

CORE EVENTS OF AN INDUSTRIAL DISASTER

by Steven Otfinoski

Consultant:
Kathryn Dowgiewicz
ILGWU Project Archivist
Kheel Center for Labor-Management
Documentation & Archives
Cornell University, Ithaca, New York

CAPSTONE PRESS
a capstone imprint

Fact Finders Books are published by Capstone Press,
1710 Roe Crest Drive, North Mankato, Minnesota 56003
www.capstonepub.com

Library of Congress Cataloging-in-Publication Data
Otfinoski, Steven.
  The Triangle Shirtwaist Factory fire : core events of an industrial disaster / by Steven Otfinoski.
    pages cm. — (Fact finders: what went wrong?)
  Includes bibliographical references and index.
  Summary: "Explains the Triangle Shirtwaist Factory fire, including its chronology, causes, and lasting
effects"— Provided by publisher.
  ISBN 978-1-4765-4183-9 (library binding) ISBN 978-1-4765-5132-6 (paperback)
  ISBN 978-1-4765-5981-0 (eBook PDF)
1. Triangle Shirtwaist Company—Fire, 1911—Juvenile literature. 2. Clothing factories—New York
(State)—New York—Safety measures—History—20th century—Juvenile literature. 3. Industrial
safety—New York (State)—New York—History—20th century—Juvenile literature. 4. New York
(N.Y.)—History—1898–1951—Juvenile literature. 5. Labor laws and legislation—New York (State)—
New York—History—20th century—Juvenile literature. I. Title.
  F128.5.O84 2014
  974.7'1041—dc23   2013025109

Editorial Credits
Jennifer Huston, editor; Bobbie Nuytten, designer; Wanda Winch, media researcher; Kathy McColley,
production specialist

Photo Credits
Brown Brothers, Sterling, PA., 9; Corbis: Underwood & Underwood, cover (bottom), 15; Getty Images
Inc: AFP/Rizwan Tabassum, 26; Kheel Center, Cornell University, cover (top), 5, 7, 8, 10, 11, 16-21;
Library of Congress: Prints and Photographs Division, 4, 6, 12, 14, 23: National Archives and Records
Administration, 13 (all); Shutterstock: Ilya Andriyanov (flames, fire), Marfot (castle design), Natutik,
grunge fire design; U.S. Fire Administration: Jack Yates, 24, 25

Primary Source Bibliography
Pages 8, 12, 14—Brooks, Tom. "The Terrible Triangle Fire." *American Heritage*, August 1957, 54–57.
Page 11—Stein, Leon. *The Triangle Fire*. ILR Press an imprint of Cornell University Press, 1962.
Page 16—Schneiderman, Rose. "We Have Found You Wanting." Originally published in *The Survey*,
        April 8, 1911, and reprinted on the Cornell University website, www.ilr.cornell.edu/
        trianglefire/.
Page 17—*The Sun*, "Panic Caused the Heavy Death Loss." March 28, 1911.
Page 18—*The World* (New York), "Mighty Host Honors the Fire's Dead." April 5, 1911.

Printed in the United States of America in Stevens Point, Wisconsin.
092013   007769WZS14

Table of Contents

CHAPTER 1
Fire!

No word can strike terror in people's hearts faster than the cry of "FIRE!" Some of the worst fires have happened in the workplace. One of the deadliest workplace fires took place at the Triangle Shirtwaist Company in New York City.

March 25, 1911, was just another Saturday for the 500 workers at the Triangle Shirtwaist factory in New York City. The mostly young women who worked there made shirtwaists—women's blouses with buttons down the front. The factory took up the top three floors of the 10-**story** Asch Building, located on the corner of Greene Street and Washington Place. By 3:00 p.m., the rest of the building was nearly empty, but the young girls at their sewing machines continued to work.

Women's blouses known as shirtwaists came in many different styles.

MAKING A LIVING

Some of the young girls who worked at the Triangle Shirtwaist factory were only 14 years old. Most of them were Italian and Jewish **immigrants**. They labored 12 hours a day and were paid only $15 a week.

story—a level of a building

immigrant—someone who comes from one country to live permanently in another country

Around 4:30 p.m., shortly before quitting time, a small fire broke out on the eighth floor. Several employees tried to put it out with buckets of water, but the blaze was soon out of control. The flames ate up the paper patterns, wooden tables, and heaps of loose material, causing the fire to spread rapidly.

ignite—to set fire to something

In the early 1900s when this photo was taken, sewing machine operators worked at long, cramped tables. Scraps of material littered the floor.

5

Run for Your Lives!

Shortly after the fire started, a worker on the eighth floor telephoned the offices on the ninth and 10th floors. But there was no answer on the ninth floor. By the time the workers on the ninth floor were aware of the fire, it was too late for most of them to escape.

Some workers on the 10th floor rushed up the Greene Street stairway to the building's roof. Students from New York University, which was located next door, heard the girls screaming for help and acted quickly.

The students positioned ladders between the two buildings and helped people climb across to the roof of the school building. Triangle co-owner Max Blanck and two of his young daughters escaped the blaze this way. But within a few minutes, the smoke and the rapidly spreading fire made the Greene Street staircase impassable. Several workers from the ninth floor died in the stairwell.

There was also a staircase on the Washington Place side of the building, but the doors to it were locked. The factory's owners had done this to prevent workers from stealing material and sneaking out to take unapproved breaks. Eventually, workers were able to force open the door on the eighth floor. Those on the ninth floor weren't as lucky.

Many of the people who died in the Triangle fire were trapped here on the ninth floor.

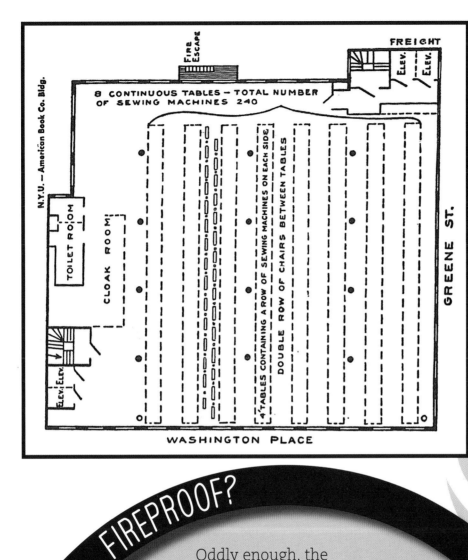

N.Y.U. — American Book Co. Bldg.

FIRE ESCAPE

FREIGHT

ELEV. ELEV.

8 CONTINUOUS TABLES — TOTAL NUMBER OF SEWING MACHINES 240

TOILET ROOM

CLOAK ROOM

4 TABLES CONTAINING A ROW OF SEWING MACHINES ON EACH SIDE

DOUBLE ROW OF CHAIRS BETWEEN TABLES

GREENE ST.

ELEV. ELEV.

WASHINGTON PLACE

This diagram shows the layout of the ninth floor of the Asch Building at the time of the fire. Many Triangle employees had to climb over several rows of tables to try to escape the blaze.

FIREPROOF?

Oddly enough, the building's owner Joseph Asch claimed that it was fireproof. This may have been true of the outer structure, but the building had wooden floors, trim, and window frames. If the building had been a story higher, concrete floors and metal trim and window frames would have been required by law. After the fire the building's outer walls and roof were still intact. Fire damaged equipment and material on the top three floors and took many lives.

Meanwhile, two brave men operating the Washington Place elevators offered another way out. Despite the danger, they made multiple trips carrying about 200 Triangle employees to safety. Finally, one of the two men fainted, and the other made a grim discovery. Frantic women who were trying to slide down the elevator shaft had slipped and fallen to their deaths. Their bodies jammed the elevator shaft and made it impossible to operate the elevator.

Joseph Zito was one of the elevator operators who helped many people safely exit the burning building.

A REPORTER'S VIEW

By 5:00 p.m., thousands of **spectators** had gathered outside the Asch Building to watch the ongoing tragedy. Among them was James Cooper, a reporter for *The World*. In the newspaper, he later wrote:

"For fully a minute the spectators seemed in doubt as to whether the smoke meant fire or was simply some unusual smoke that might come from a machine … Within another minute the entire eighth floor was spouting little jets of flame from the windows as if the floor was surrounded by a row of … lights."

A fire escape facing Greene Street was the only other way out. But the heat from the **fiery** blaze twisted and bent the metal staircase out of shape. The weight from all the people rushing down the fire escape caused it to collapse. At least 20 people fell to their deaths. At that point, those still in the building—mostly on the ninth floor—were hopelessly trapped.

The intense heat from the Triangle factory fire caused the Greene Street fire escape to collapse.

spectator—a person who watches an event

fiery—being on fire

No one knows for sure how the fire started. The fire chief later said he believed that a spark from a cigarette ignited a bin of rags.

Although it is uncertain *how* the fire started, there's no doubt what caused it to spread so quickly. The fire chief said he believed gasoline—which was used in irons for pressing the shirts—fueled the fire. Between the gasoline, the oil-soaked machines, and all the loose material in the room, the fire was quickly out of control.

Narrow staircases prevented more fire victims from safely exiting the building.

A Hopeless Cause

Even though there were multiple ways to exit the burning building, many workers found themselves trapped inside. Locked doors, narrow, smoke-filled staircases, and a broken fire escape certainly caused many preventable deaths. But other factors also played a role.

Nellie Ventura was one of the lucky survivors of the Triangle fire. She made it down the fire escape before it collapsed.

"At first I was too frightened to try to run through the fire. Then I heard the screams of the girls inside. I knew I had to go down the ladder or die where I was."

A large crowd watches as firefighters try to put out the blaze at the Asch Building.

Firefighters arrived in time to save more people from the blaze, but their efforts failed. Why? There were several reasons. First, more than 50 desperate women and men jumped from the building's windows. They took the risk of jumping and possibly surviving the fall rather than face certain death in the blaze. But the life nets used to catch falling victims proved useless. Many people helped firefighters hold the enormous nets, but it made little difference. When several women jumped together, the tremendous force of their falling bodies ripped the nets from the rescuers' hands. The victims struck the pavement and died instantly.

A horse-drawn fire engine races to the scene of the Triangle factory fire.

"The bodies didn't break through the nets; they just carried them to the sidewalk. The force was so great it took the men off their feet ... The men turned somersaults over onto the bodies."
—Fire Captain Howard Ruch

Firefighters carry away a victim who landed on their hoses after jumping from the Triangle factory.

Most of them fell nearly 100 feet (30 meters) to their deaths. Some of the bodies landed on the firefighters' hoses. Others piled up and blocked the street. This pile of dead bodies made it difficult for firefighters to do their work.

Onlookers watch as frantic fire victims prepare to jump to their deaths like those laying on the sidewalk did.

DID YOU KNOW?

The bodies falling from the Asch Building struck the sidewalk with a force of 11,000 pounds (4,990 kilograms).

Another factor that fueled the disaster was the firefighters' ladders. The ladders were only long enough to reach the sixth floor of the Asch Building, but the fire was two stories above that.

Within 40 minutes after the blaze started, it was over. The final death toll was 146. About 50 people died from burns or **suffocation** from smoke. The rest perished from falling down the elevator shaft or leaping to their deaths out the windows. As the smoke cleared, New Yorkers were shaken and shocked by the tragedy. It didn't take long for them to question who was responsible and what had caused this terrible disaster.

"A girl's clothes caught on fire, and a man's, and they jumped. I [saw] one girl run to a window, and when I got down to the sidewalk, I had to step over her."
—Survivor Rose Bernstein

A police officer looks at the fire damage on the ninth floor.

suffocation—to die from lack of oxygen

Triangle Shirtwaist Factory Fire Timeline

March 25, 1911: around 4:30 p.m.: Fire breaks out on the eighth floor of the Asch Building in New York City, home of the Triangle Shirtwaist Company.

March 25, 1911: around 5:10 p.m.: Firefighters put out the fire. The death toll is 146.

April 5, 1911: More than 100,000 factory workers march up Fifth Avenue to mourn and remember the Triangle factory fire victims.

June 30, 1911: The New York Factory Investigating Commission is established to investigate working conditions in the city's factories.

December 4, 1911: The trial of Triangle Shirtwaist Company owners Isaac Harris and Max Blanck begins.

December 27, 1911: Harris and Blanck are found not guilty. This verdict causes a public uproar.

1915: The Investigating Commission ends its work. State lawmakers pass 36 of the laws the commission proposed.

Despite the tragic loss of lives, some good did come out of the Triangle factory fire. Lawmakers were forced to find solutions to the problems of unsafe and dangerous working conditions in which many Americans toiled.

Public Outrage

The public was shocked and angry at the unnecessary loss of life at the Triangle Shirtwaist factory. The public's anger led to action. People demanded that something be done to improve working conditions and prevent future workplace disasters like the Triangle factory fire.

On April 2 a memorial meeting was held at the Metropolitan Opera House. There, labor **union** leader and **feminist** Rose Schneiderman spoke to hundreds of garment workers. In her speech, Schneiderman said:

> *"… I know from my experience it is up to the working people to save themselves. The only way they can save themselves is by a strong working class movement."*

Rose Schneiderman

Other protests and demonstrations were held across the city. People spoke out against factory owners who forced people to work in unsafe conditions.

union—an organized group of workers set up to help improve such things as working conditions, wages, and health benefits

feminist—someone who believes strongly that women ought to have the same opportunities and rights that men have

"Here we have a building, fireproof in the eyes of the law and a building in which apparently all legal requirements were met … [W]hat we need is a bureau of fire prevention … with power to make changes which would provide for the actual safety of people living or working in such buildings. A fire drill might have prevented this terrible thing, and yet there is no one with authority in this whole city to demand such a thing of factory owners."

—Fire Marshal William Beers,
The Sun, March 28, 1911

Protesters demand better working conditions in the city's factories.

On April 5, 1911, more than 100,000 factory workers marched up Fifth Avenue to honor the Triangle factory fire victims. About 300,000 people watched the sad event, which lasted for several hours in the pouring rain. Marchers from the Ladies Waist and Dressmakers Union carried a black banner that read "We Mourn Our Loss."

"Today's demonstration was like nothing that has gone before. The ... dead ... were of the humblest type. They were born to toil and died at their work. It was this that made the parade most remarkable."

—*The World*, Evening Edition, April 5, 1911

Thousands of people came out for the funeral procession of several unidentified victims who died in the Triangle fire.

Seeking Justice

In December 1911, Isaac Harris and Max Blanck, the owners of the Triangle Shirtwaist Company, were put on trial for the deaths of the fire victims. They were blamed for the locked doors that prevented victims from escaping the burning building.

More than 150 witnesses—most of them Triangle employees—testified that the Washington Place doors were locked on the eighth and ninth floors. But the judge told the jury members that they had to decide beyond a reasonable doubt whether the owners knew the doors were locked. Despite the evidence against Harris and Blanck, it took the jury only two hours to find them not guilty.

Triangle Shirtwaist Company owners Max Blanck (left) and Isaac Harris (right) were found not guilty of the deaths in the fire at their factory.

State lawmakers were determined to find a solution to the problem of workplace disasters like the Triangle factory fire. They appointed a group to investigate working conditions. The investigation took four years. Of the many suggestions they made to increase workplace safety, 36 of their ideas were enacted into law. These new laws required buildings to be fireproofed. They also required that fire alarms, **fire extinguishers**, and hoses be installed in all buildings. These laws were the strictest of their kind in the nation and became a model for other states.

In 1909 Clara Lemlich led thousands of garment workers in a strike. They demanded better working conditions, fair wages, and shorter hours.

Ironically, many of the workers who lost their lives in the Triangle fire had gone on strike in 1909. At the time, they had been fighting with management and factory owners for workers' rights and safer working conditions. After the fire, workers' unions, particularly the International Ladies' Garment Workers' Union (ILGWU), swelled in membership. They fought hard to make sure that one of the worst workplace tragedies in U.S. history resulted in a better future for all American workers.

fire extinguisher—a device that holds chemicals to spray on small fires

Nearly two years before the tragedy at the Triangle factory, the city's garment workers protested the unsafe conditions in which they worked.

The Triangle Shirtwaist factory fire ranks fourth among the deadliest industrial accidents in U.S. history. But in comparison, some other workplace tragedies are just as compelling.

Pemberton Mill Disaster

The Pemberton Mill disaster in Lawrence, Massachusetts, was almost as deadly as the Triangle Shirtwaist factory fire. However, unlike the Triangle disaster, this one didn't start as a fire. On January 10, 1860, the old five-story factory building simply collapsed, trapping about 600 workers inside. Rescuers were able to save many of the workers, but then an overturned lantern started a fire in the ruins. Those still trapped were burned alive. The final death toll was 145, just one less than the count in the Triangle factory fire.

One hundred forty-five people died in the Pemberton Mill disaster when a building collapsed then caught fire.

Imperial Foods Fire

In September 1991 a frying machine at the Imperial Foods chicken processing plant in North Carolina caught fire. Like the Triangle Shirtwaist factory fire, several emergency exit doors were locked or blocked. Managers locked them so that workers couldn't sneak out with pieces of chicken. That left only two ways to escape the building. Twenty-five people died before they could get out. Fifty-six others were injured.

Workers trapped inside the burning Imperial Foods factory tried to kick open the padlocked doors. Their blackened footprints are seen here.

In the 11 years that the factory had been opened, state safety officials had never inspected it. An investigation after the fire found the factory's owners guilty of 83 violations that endangered the safety of employees. Unlike the Triangle fire, the company owner, Emmett Roe, was found guilty for these deaths. The company was fined more than $800,000 for breaking safety laws, and Roe was sentenced to 19 years in prison. He only served four and a half years before he was released.

It is believed that the fire at the Imperial Foods factory started at a chicken fryer in the kitchen.

Pakistan's Garment Factory Fire

One of the worst factory fires in history took place at Ali Enterprises in Pakistan, on September 11, 2012. Similar to the Triangle Shirtwaist factory, Ali Enterprises also made clothing. It is unknown how the fire started.

These men inspect the damage at Ali Enterprises where nearly 300 people died in a fire in 2012.

The fire at Ali Enterprises raged for 12 hours. Nearly 300 people were killed—more than twice as many as in the Triangle factory fire. Like the Triangle fire, emergency exit doors were locked. Even worse, most of the windows had bars on them. People leaped from the top floors to escape the flames and smoke. The building was only four stories high, so some of the jumpers in the Pakistan blaze survived the fall. None of those at the Triangle factory did.

The owners of Ali Enterprises were charged with murder, but the charges were later reduced to **negligence**.

An Unforgettable Tragedy

Why is the Triangle Shirtwaist factory fire better known than these other disasters? First, its horrible events took place in the largest city in the United States as thousands of New Yorkers watched helplessly. And at the time, it was the deadliest industrial accident in the city's history. It also prompted lawmakers to take notice and pass laws to make all workplaces safer. Most importantly, many of the deaths in this terrible tragedy could have been prevented.

negligence—the act of being careless or not attentive to one's duties

	Pemberton Mill Disaster **January 10, 1860**	Triangle Shirtwaist Factory Fire **March 25, 1911**
Location	Lawrence, Massachusetts	New York City
How the fire started	Overturned lantern following a building collapse	Exact cause unknown, but possibly from a cigarette tossed in a bin of rags
What went wrong?	Those who were trapped in the rubble of the collapsed building died from the smoke and flames.	Locked exit doors trapped many people inside the burning building.
Number of deaths	145	146

Imperial Foods Factory Fire **September 3, 1991**	Ali Enterprises **September 11, 2012**
Hamlet, North Carolina	Karachi, Pakistan
Exact cause unknown, but possibly from a chicken fryer	Exact cause unknown, but it may have been due to an electrical short circuit
Doors were locked or blocked. As a result, many people were unable to escape the blaze.	The doors were locked and the windows had bars over them, trapping many people inside the building.
25	Nearly 300

DID YOU KNOW?

The building where the Triangle factory fire took place still exists. It is now part of New York University. NYU students attend classes in the same building where so many people tragically lost their lives.

Glossary

feminist (FEM-uh-nist): someone who believes strongly that women ought to have the same opportunities and rights that men have

fiery (FYE-ree): being on fire

fire extinguisher (FYR ik-STING-gwi-shur): a device that holds chemicals to spray on small fires

ignite (ig-NITE): to set fire to something

immigrant (IM-uh-gruhnt): someone who comes from one country to live permanently in another country

negligence (NEG-luh-juhns): the act of being careless or not attentive to one's duties

spectator (SPEK-tay-tur): a person who watches an event

story (STOR-ee): a level of a building

suffocate (SUHF-uh-kate): to die from lack of oxygen

union (YOON-yuhn): an organized group of workers set up to help improve such things as working conditions, wages, and health benefits

Internet Sites

FactHound offers a safe, fun way to find Internet sites related to this book. All of the sites on FactHound have been researched by our staff.

Here's all you do:

Visit *www.facthound.com*

Type in this code: 9781476541839

Super-cool stuff!

Check out projects, games and lots more at **www.capstonekids.com**

Critical Thinking Using the Common Core

1. Why were so many workers unable to escape from the fire at the Triangle Shirtwaist factory? (Key Ideas and Details)

2. Many people were angry about the conditions that caused the Triangle factory fire. Name some of the ways in which that anger led to changes in working conditions. (Key Ideas and Details)

3. Look at the diagram on page 7 that shows the layout of the ninth floor of the Asch Building. How does it help to explain what happened when the fire started and began to spread? (Craft and Structure)

Read More

Getzinger, Donna. *Triangle Shirtwaist Factory Fire*. American Workers. Greensboro, N.C.: Morgan Reynolds Publishing, 2009.

Greene, Jacqueline Dembar. *The Triangle Shirtwaist Factory Fire*. Code Red. New York: Bearport, 2007.

Nobleman, Marc Tyler. *The Triangle Shirtwaist Factory Fire*. We the People. Minneapolis: Compass Point Books, 2008.

Index